Norway

Travel Norway Like a Local

W. Johnson

Contents

Chapter 1: Introducing Norway

"The greatest secrets are always hidden in the most unlikely places. Those who don't believe in magic will never find it." – Roald Dahl

Norway is a smorgasbord of magic. It is remarkably simple in its languid pace yet one of the grandest places on earth. The magnificence of Norway's natural landscape is impossible to overstate. The land hosts everything from dramatically steep fjords (yes the word fjord itself sounds grand) to jagged coastlines to icefields to the once-in-a lifetime Northern lights experience – there are few places on earth that are as interesting primeval (ice lands, reindeers, musk oxen, wooden villages and more) as effortlessly contemporary.

Complement the natural fortresses and rocky islands featuring interiors with Norway's cosmopolitan cities, brimming with architecture and culture and you have a hard to resist potpourri. The Scandinavian penchant for design is evident throughout its monuments and everyday structures. Not content with being a mere visual fest, Norway's calendar of events is choc-o-bloc with a variety of festivals.

Norway can be one of the priciest travel destinations on earth, which is why it is considered more like a lifetime trip. Is it worth saving to make a trip to Norway? An astounding yes! Norway will give you back multifold in the form of unforgettable memories, culture and experiences.

The primary attraction in Norway is its vast and indisputably beautiful countryside landscape, replete with islands, forests, mountains, lakes, fjords, waterfalls and the iconic fjords. Even their national anthem offers an ode to the nations "ruggedness" in its opening lines. One of the biggest mistakes tourists in Norway make is to simply dash from city to city in the pursuit of interesting experiences. Make no mistake – Norway has some of the most culturally fascinating and visually stunning metros(Oslo, Bergen). However, its real treasures lay hidden in castaway rural districts.

Norway most emphatically cannot be experienced by making a trip to a couple of handpicked Norwegian cities. The nation's distinct charm, unlike several other touristy places, cannot be limited to a few attractions pinned on a map. Almost everything on the route is an attraction in Norway. Its most monumentally attractive landscapes are not housed in packed national parks but tucked away somewhere in the most unknown regions. Norway fittingly rewards travelers who are enthusiastic enough to uncover its hidden beauty in the form of unfading travel memories. It is best to enjoy Norway's natural and cultural splendor on more adaptable and generous schedules. Slow down and savor Norway to truly experience it!

Being one of the most prosperous countries on earth, Norway can be particularly expensive in personal service related purchases such as taxis and eating out. One good thing here is the mentioned price often includes VAT and service taxes, which gives you a fair idea about the final tally. However, if you are a bells and whistles free traveler who loves the sheer ruggedness of exploring a country, the best things in Norway, just as in life, are all free. There are no fees for accessing its wilderness zones, beaches (even the privately owned ones) and certain state owned national galleries. Good reason to hop on a public transport rather than a private taxi? You bet. If you are resourceful and locally savvy (which you most likely will be at the end of this book), there's a lot you can do and see without robbing a bank.

Did you know that according to the Norwegian "right to access", you can skimp on accommodation by living on a uncultivated patch of land for a couple of nights, provided you are away from other houses and not in people's way and leave absolutely no trace? Travelers can often be spotted sleeping below the night sky or holed up in a tent to enjoy the wilderness of the region on a tight budget. Visitors who manage to access uninhabited regions can live there until they are permitted to be in Norway.

Another plus for outsiders is that Norway boasts of extremely high standards when it comes to health, hygiene and safety. The tap water found everywhere here is not just drinkable but also of remarkably high quality (beats even bottled water). As long as you don't mess with its natural forces and exercise caution where more accidents occur (ocean, waterfalls, glaciers etc), you are good in Norway.

Norway lies in the extreme North but thankfully doesn't feature an arctic climate. Bergen (located in south west coastal region) showcases a more humid weather, a la Netherlands or Great Britain. The eastern destinations (Oslo and others) typically offer a more continental weather, with balmy summers (20-30 degrees C). Rain is more of a challenge for summer visitors than the biting cold climate.

Watch out for the Nordic sun in mountainous regions, snow lands and water bodies – it is known to cause grave skin burns. It is a good idea to always have a pair of UV-filter sunglasses handy while travelling in summers. Daylight appears to last forever in summers, and temperatures are exceeding pleasant. The skiing season is at its peak from November to April though a few resorts also are only operational from May to September.

It is important to note that the weather varies considerably between different Norwegian regions. Driving for a couple hours may lead you from a frosty destination to a mildly pleasant one. Since most major cities in Norway are located in close proximity to the ocean, they enjoy the warmer winds of the Gulf Stream. Visitors should avoid driving (unless extremely experienced) during winters from November to March, when the mountainous regions experience intense snowfall. Mountain passes are sometimes shut summarily when there's massive snowfall. Though winter is said to end in March, April still has some northern and inland regions engulfed by the cold climate. Spring commences mostly on May, and can be one of the best times for winter-phobes to experience Norway. Snow bodies seeking winter adventures in Norway can plan trips during December to April.

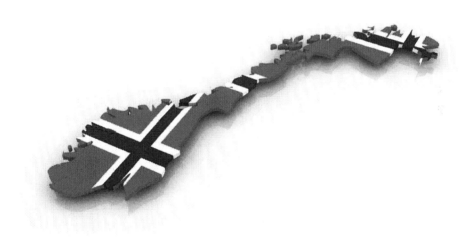

The best time to go hiking on Norway's rugged country paths is during July to August, since the central mountain districts are brimming with snow. The coast regions housed on lower attitudes feature a more extended hiking period. Even in summers, mountainous regions have temperatures plunging to 1 degree C. per 100-150 meters altitude raise.

Though Norway's restaurants can be significantly expensive for visitors, its supermarkets can offer decent value for money on a variety of food products. Moral of the story – you will save a lot by cooking your own meals. Rema and Kiwi are popular budget supermarkets. Another treasure trove for reasonably priced meals are Norway's bakeries. You can lay your hands on everything from over-fresh breads to savory pastries to sandwiches and cakes. Pizzerias though varying in food standards are other little known eating hide outs for travelers. This is where you go when you want to "fill up" on an empty pocket. A pizza can cost anywhere between 120-150 NOK, where restaurant meals can tally up to NOK 200-290.

If there's one thing travelers come in search of in Norway, it is indisputably the fjords. They are the country's biggest natural attractions, with tourists jostling to capture their beauty at the UNESCO protected Geiranger and Flam. Fjords are Norway's predominant attribute right from its Western regions (Stavanger) to the northern belt (Tromso). The beauty of witnessing these fjords is you don't have to go to any single destination to view them. They are everywhere, along most western and northern routes. Fit them into your overall itinerary in such a way that you don't need to make frequent and pointless detours just to see the more popular ones.

The midnight sun is another quintessentially Norwegian phenomenon. It can be witnessed anywhere to the North of Bodo around summer. North Cape isn't the only place where you can experience the grandeur of the famed midnight sun, since its effects are notable evident further down south as well. Southern Norwegian mid summers features extremely brief nights, often fittingly referred as "white nights." In Oslo you can comfortably read outdoor during midnight. The midnight sun experience can be included as add on to your northern Norway landscape itinerary. The world famous northern lights (aurora borealis) manifest in the winter months at higher altitudes in the northern regions but can also be spotted down south.

The coastal regions, comprising fjords and mountains, feature highly complex topography. Public transport is generally restricted to a single bus operating within a 24 hour span. Therefore, Norway just cannot be witnessed in a short time. If you are making shorter trips, you will do well to focus only on specific cities or regions. Travelling between regions and cities can be an all-consuming affair, given the weather and tricky detours. Travelling from north to south requires several days. Several vacationers come to Norway on a tight schedule with an elaborate travel plan without taking into consideration weather uncertainties, unpredictable transport and treacherous routes, especially during winters. Sketch rough travel plans by weaving more flexible schedules into them.

How north is too north in Norway? Alesund and Lofoten Islands, other than northernmost point of North Cape are recommended options for those seeking the famed natural glory of the Nordic north. Trondheim is another good option, while Svalbard is for the more intrepid explorers. The pace of Norway is tailor made for independent travelers. Lots of space, long distances, adventure-packed routes and an efficiently organized (though influenced by erratic weather conditions) transport system make Norway a backpacker's paradise.

For a country inhabited by less than 5 million residents, Norway is fairly large and refreshingly sparse. Its mainland region covers about 15 degrees from north to south. Norway's southernmost tip to the Russian border spans about 3000 kilometers. Norway's mainland is thrice as long as Germany, and the nation is a little smaller than California but again thrice as long. The nation's cumulative coastline is a staggering 25,000 kilometers, including the islands. Owing to its incredible length distance, it is both a western as well as eastern European nation. The farthest mainland eastern town is even further than St. Petersburg and Istanbul, while Bergen is located further than Cologne and Milano.

The Norwegians' enthusiasm for exploring their world class natural resources has transformed the country into one of the most sought after eco and adventure tourism destinations. This is the land of the energetic and plucky – think world class white water rafting, dog sledding, snowmobiling, skiing, cycling and more. Whether you head to Norway to enjoy its pleasant summers (or the famous midnight sun) or its seemingly endless winters (the soul simulating northern lights), there are plenty of nature-adventure based activities to keep visitors exhilarated. Marked by a combination of the signature Scandinavian sophistication and irresistible ruggedness of the primeval ice-age, Norway scores all the way.

Norway's indigenous Sami folks inhabit the country's northern areas, which along with regions of Finland, Russia and Sweden form the Sapmi outline area. A majority of Norway's inhabitants are Norwegians, though there has been a considerable influx of immigrants in recent years, mostly from the European Union.

Norwegians have for long battled harsh climatic conditions, which has made them laborious and intensely individualistic. They are friendly, gentle and hospitable, but can be misunderstood as cold for their non-acceptance of change or characteristic skepticism. Since their circles are so close knit, Norwegians do not trust people easily or jump into friendships. However, once they get to know you well, the bond is solid and amiable.

Though 85% of the Norwegians were disciples of the national church, in 2012 the government broke away from the church, which left Norway with no official religion. Like its Scandinavian neighbors, Norway is fairly liberal when it comes to issues related to morality and sexuality. In 2008, same sex marriages attained legal status. There are still some southern regions (especially rural areas), which harbor a more conservative attitude; though on the whole Norway is more liberal and noninterventionist.

Being one of the world's wealthiest countries with a stable economy, Norway's purchasing capacity per capita is notably higher than the European Union and the US. They have a very condensed wage model, which makes even low skilled jobs well paying. Norway's primarily Scandinavian revenue model comprising high taxes and increased government sponsored education, healthcare, welfare system and more has worked wonderfully well for Norway. The country's unemployment is pegged at a mere 2 percent. While the fundamental sources of its economy are gas and oil from the North Sea, there are other natural resources (minerals and fish) to bolster the country's economy.

Chapter 2: Oslo

Oslo is the avant-garde artistic child of Norway. Featuring a luxuriant natural canvas, the city is a heady assortment of distinguished museums, art galleries and architectural masterpieces. However, Oslo is not merely limited to all things artistic, and is bountifully fringed by Norway's signature natural beauty in the form of forests, lush hills and lakes that offer perfect boating and cycling opportunities. Add a flourishing café scene, world-class restaurants, a buzzing bar culture and myriad nightlife options, and you have a place that can endearingly mystifying and enjoyable all the same. If you want to take a break from the fjords and ice, by all means let Oslo be your host. Here's how to negotiate the place like an insider.

Oslo Attractions

Akershus Fortress

Akershus Fortress is a good starting point for getting acquainted with the Oslo's past or just about enjoying a lazy summer day. The Akershus Castle was commissioned by king Hakon V in 1299, and is famous for surviving several siege attempts through history. During the 16th-17th century, King Christian IV gave the castle a more contemporary demeanor, and transformed it into a Renaissance period royal castle. During summers, visitors can enjoy guided tours of the fortress. The heritage structure is also a celebrated venue for concerts, holiday celebrations and grand local ceremonies.

Aker Brygge

Aker Brygge is the soul of Oslo. The iconic and architecturally stunning attraction pays a fitting homage is Norway's philosophy of embracing the new without letting go of its roots. It seamlessly blends the modern and traditional, and is visited by about 12 million people annually. Little wonder, given its potpourri of patio bars, fine dine restaurants, discerning shops and stylish sea-front promenade. Hop into the Astrup Fernly Museum of Modern Art while you are here. It features a nice collection of permanent works (Jeff Koons, Andy Warhol and others) and rotating exhibits.

Vigeland Sculpture Park

The biggest park of its kind on earth, Vigeland Sculpture Park houses Gustav Vigeland's works of art in the form of over 600 granite, iron and bronze sculptures. He designed the layout and façade of the park including a fountain group (that pays tribute to the human life cycle) and a lofty 55 ft. Monolith (holding 121 human bodies). Art, design and architecture buffs will devour the maverick artistic creations of Vigeland.

Oslo Cathedral

Though it was sanctified in the 17th century, Oslo's cathedral has witnessed several renovations and repairs. The most eminent features of the edifice include its intricate bronze doors and H. L. Mohr's extraordinarily beautiful ceiling paintings. Emanuel Vigeland's deft stain glass patterns are also worth a mention. After a walk through the cathedral, head to Oslo Bazaar, located alongside the erstwhile church walls. The halls are a bustling hodge-podge of art galleries, antique stores and cafés.

Royal Palace

Built in the early 19th century, The Royal Palace is housed at the northwestern tip of Karl Johansgate. Though the palace per se is not open to visitors, the public is allowed to access its grounds and garden premises. You can even witness the intriguing guard changing procedure. The Norwegian Nobel Institute (yes, the one that presents Nobel Peace Prize) is located just South of the Royal Palace.

Natural History Museum and Botanical Gardens

The National History Museum and Botanical Garden is the country's largest collection of natural history in the form of dinosaur skeletons, precious metals, minerals and much more. The museum is split into a Geological Museum, Botanical Gardens and a Zoological Museum, where visitors can saunter around at a leisurely pace. The highlight here is the verdant 19th century botanical gardens that house over 7000 varied indigenous and global plant species. Visit the rock garden which houses about 1,500 plants and an ethereal looking waterfall.

Viking Museum

This one's for all those Viking history and culture buffs. It features a trio of the country's most significant treasures in the form of the

Tune, Oseberg and Gokstad Viking ship. Did you know the burial ships were crammed with clothing, food, jewelry and more before the Vikings believed their chieftains and other distinguished citizens would need all those items in their next life? The modest sized museum can be covered in less than a couple of hours. You may justify the high ticket price considering the elaborate process of excavating the 19th century ships from burial sites, encasing them in rocks and clay and educating interested visitors by explaining the entire restoration process. To sum it up –if you're a Viking culture and history fan, you will smack yourself hard on the head for missing this.

One of the most cost effective ways to visit Norway's museums is to grab the Oslo passes that are commonly available at most tourist inhabited places including the city's tourist information offices, major hotels and some museums. The passes can be purchased for a 24, 36 and 48 hour period for 36, 53 and 67 EU respectively for adults. Passes for kids and seniors are priced at 18, 27 and 33 EU for 24,48 and 72 hours respectively.

City Hall (Radhuset)

Oslo's gargantuan City Hall is one of Norway's most distinguished landmarks. The commanding square structure erected out of brick and concrete features two towers, with one of them holding an imposing clock. One of these fascinating towers holds 38 bells, whose haunting chimes echo all over the harbor region. There are lots of other intriguing facades and sculptures, along with fresco-laden interiors created by a bunch of noteworthy Norwegian artists.

Oslo Opera House

The Oslo Opera House is the focal point of an ambitious waterfront urban redevelopment project that is slated to go on until 2020. Costing a whopping €500 million, the 2008 launched structure is modeled to look like a floating glacier on Oslo's balmy waters. While it's easy to think of the edifice as tourist eye candy, there are a number of fine ballet and opera renditions hosted here. Join the Norwegian and English guided tours that let you discover the venue's 1000 plus rooms and fascinating behind the curtains trivia. Ticket prices vary from NOK 100 to NOK 745.

Normarka

Oslo may probably be the sole capital on planet earth to have a wild forest bang in the middle of its city life. While Tryvan Vinterpark is a skier's manna from heaven, the Tryvannstartnet tower is a great starting point for a hiking or biking expedition. Lots of blueberries dotting the ground in summers so make sure you carry something to collect them. Enjoy a picturesque ride from Hokmenkollen to Frognerseteren and keep your eyes open for the walking route signpost at the far end of the Frognerseteren line.

Damstredet

Want to have a peak-a-boo of Oslo's erstwhile 18th century elegant wooden houses? Damstredet and Telthusbakken are a refreshing break from the city's contemporary landscape. Once a shanty town for the city's destitute, Damstret is a popular hotbed for local artists. Walk straight north of the Akersgata and take a right turn on Danstredet. You'll also pass the Var Frelsers Gavlund , where Munch and Ibsen are buried.

Holmenkollen Ski Jump and Museum

The Holmenkollen Ski Jump offers sweeping views of Oslo, while also acting a stunning concert venue. Come March and the attraction transforms into a buzzing swarm of skiers from all the over participating in the annual ski festival. Even if you are not a plucky ski jumper, the venue is worth visiting for its interesting ski museum and a handful of other attractions. There is a sky jump simulator right outside the ski jump tower (accessed via lift and climbing the last 114 stairs yourself), which should skipped by the more faint hearted.

TusenFryd

Locate 10 kilometers to the south of Oslo; TusenFryd is hugely popular with children and with good reason. The park features fascinating carousels, a make-believe farm and an impressive zero gravity a dozen times each circuit wooden rollercoaster. Take a bus (no 546) from Fred Olsens gate and Prinsens gate every hour from 10am to 4pm to get here.

Hop-on Hop-Off City Sightseeing Tours

Explore the most summery Scandinavian capital by taking an enjoyable city sightseeing hop-on hop-off bus tour. The cute top open double decker buses offer panoramic views of the city's most prominent attractions. For a single day price, you can hop on and off about 17 easily accessible stops. The sightseeing is sprinkled with interesting commentary. The complete route is covered in about 90 minutes, and there's a bus every half hour. Tickets come with 24-hour validity.

Oslo Mini Cruise
Witness the breathtakingly appeal of Oslo's waterfront on a sightseeing cruise. The 90-minute trip takes visitors through a host of the city's popular attractions such as the Oslo Opera House, Akershus fortress and a bunch of Bygdoy peninsula museums. This is a relatively fast and cheap way to experience Oslofjord. The cruise features onboard audio commentary about the tourist attractions, as you pass them.

Dipping Into the Pool
There are plenty of islands around Oslo that are ideal for lazy beach bumming and swimming. Ferries take enthusiastic beachcombers from Oslo's city center to neighboring islands. Some of the beaches that can be conveniently accessed from Oslo include Huk, Katten, Bygdoy and Ingierstrand. Sorenga has a new harbor bath, where holiday revelers can be spotted frolicking in the waters.

For fresh water dipping, Akerselva to the north of Nydalen is a clean and pleasant spot. There are a cluster of lakes in Oslomarka, which are perfect for swimming, family picnics and recreation. These pools can be reached via public transport buses from Oslo's city center.

Visit Grunerlokka
Probably Oslo's best kept local secret, Grunerlokka is teaming with cafes, fashion boutiques, specialty shops, sprawling parks and bars. The Akerselva River snakes on the western wide, featuring a selection of the city's strategically hidden clubs and bars. The famous Mathallen food market and Vulkan real estate development

(with its fine selection of café, offices and hotels) is nestled near the river running from Grunerlokka.

Getting Around Oslo

Like other Scandinavian nations, Oslo features refined public transport facilities which comprise buses, underground trains (also referred to as T-bane), ferries and trams. Apart from the single-trip fare tickets, visitors can also purchase a one-day or eight-trip ticket. Kids from 4-16 years of age and seniors over 67 of age are charged half the fare price.

If you plan to stick around the city for long, it makes sense to grab an Oslo Pass. It not just offers you complimentary entry in over 30 city museums but also a string of other benefits including free public transport travel, free entry to public swimming pools, free car parking in public car parks, complimentary walking tours, discounts on major attractions, bike rentals and concert tickets, and special discounts in restaurants, leisure venues, shopping and entertainment.

With the exception of mid night buses/trams and a majority of the ferries, access to all other public transport is free. Get a free public transport map and schedule from Trafikaten, housed just below Oslo S tower.

To and Fro Gardermoen Airport

Flybussen, departing from the Galleri Oslo bus terminal, is the Gardermoen International Airport (50 kilometers to the North of Oslo) shuttle. It halts at a handful of other stops every 20 minutes from about 4am to 10pm. Timings may vary. The one-way and return fare for adults is NOK 160 and 250 respectively, while for children it is NOK 80 and 160 for a single and return journey respectively. Tickets are valid for a month, and a single journey typically takes about 40 minutes.

Flybussekspressen links Gardermoen with Majorstuen T-bane station and other destinations twice to four times hourly. Buses ply from the city center airport from 4am until 8.30pm.

FlyToget rail runs between Gardermoen airport to Oslo S every 10 minutes from 4:40 am to midnight. Trains conclude at the Drammen, while stopping at the south of National Theatre. Apart from this most north-headed NSB intercity and city trains halt at Gardermoen.

To and Fro Torp Airport
Hop on the Torp Expressen bus that runs between Galleri Oslo and the airport to travel to and fro the Torp Airport (Sandefjord 123 kilometers to the southwest of Oslo). Buses leaves the city around 3 ½ hours prior to check-in shuts. Again, they leave about 35-40 minutes after the arrival of a flight. NSB trains ply between Oslo S and Torp station hourly. A shuttle bus takes travelers from the local trains to the airport (no additional fee, price included in the train ticket).

To and Fro Rygge Airport

Ryggae is the city's newest airport, located 60 km from the southeast of Oslo. Hop aboard the Ryggae-Expressen bus plying between Galleri Oslo terminal and the Rygge Airport. The bus leaves Oslo every three hours prior to a scheduled flight and leaves the airport about 35 minutes after arrival. Trains operate from Oslo S to the Rygge Airport every hour.

Buses and Trams

Oslo features an efficiently connected network of business and trams going all the way to its suburbs. Though there is no official central bus station, a majority of the local buses gather at Jernbanetorget just opposite Oslo S. Most west-headed local buses also halt at the National Theatre. The service frequency drops considerably at night, though weekend night buses (N12, N14 and

N18) follow tram routes until 4am. There are a bunch of weekend nightly buses as well (201 to 218).

Buy tickets for zone 1(comprises most of the city center routes) at a sales point (7-Eleven, Trafikanten, Narvesen and ticket machine) to save on fare. Sales point bought tickets costs NOK 30/15 for adults/kids, while those purchased on the bus or tram cost 50/25. Oslo Pass allows visitors to access all city center daytime bus/tram lines for free.

T-Bane

The six line T-Bane (Tunnelbanen) underground network offers a speedier and more extended transport system from the city center than many bus lines. All T-Bane lines move through Nationaltheatret, Storinget and Jernbanetorget for the Oslo S stations. Tickets can be purchased at 7-Eleven, ticket machine, Trafikanten and Narvesen for NOK 30 /15 for adults/kids.

Taxis

There are taxi stands all around the place at Oslo S, prominent city squares and shopping centers. Other than these stands, any taxi with a conspicuous lit sign is available for hire. Call Oslo Taxi or Norgetaxi to book taxis, though keep in mind that the meter commences from the taxi's dispatch point. All major credit cards are accepted by Oslo taxis.

Cars and Bicycles

Oslo can be slightly complicated for new drivers as it comprises many one-way streets. However, on the upside, the roads are not overcrowded like most European metros. Metered street parking can be spotted all through the city. It is indicated with a prominent blue and white P sign. Between 8am to 5pm from Monday to Friday and until 3pm on Saturdays, parking is paid. Free parking at all other times unless otherwise mentioned. Oslo's city center features 16 multilevel car parks. Parking fees can be anywhere between NOK 230 to NOK 260 for every 24 hour period. The Oslo Pass includes free parking at all municipal parking lots.

Boats

Ferries sail from Vippentangen Quay to Oslofjord islands. Boat no. 62 (commences from Aker Brygge pier) links Oslo with Drobak and a handful of other Oslofjord stops along the route such as Ildjernet,

Langara and Haova (known for its swimming and holiday camping facilities).

Travelling With Children

Dark and long winters do not see too many people on the streets; however come spring and locals enthusiastically converge on city streets with baby carriages. Oslo is not one of the most child friendly European cities, which is evident in its primarily catering to adults restaurants and tourist sites. Keep in mind that most museums and art galleries ask you to use their baby carriages, which can be a good breather for you. Oslo can still be enjoyed with children if you know where to look and head more for the open spaces rather than restaurants and more touristy venues.

Most activities that can be enjoyed with children in Oslo are free. Kids can run around the Frognerperken's mosaic maze or climb statues. The park also boasts of one of Oslo's most sprawling playgrounds. Stroll around the cannons and fascinating fortifications to stimulate your little one's imagination at Akershus Fortress. The Norwegian Folk Museum hosts regular events for children.

Eating Out

Oslo is the breeding ground of Michelin star eateries and upscale fine dining options offering everything from authentic Norwegian treats to Japanese fare to traditional Ethiopian cuisine. As mentioned earlier, prices at restaurants can be steep for travelers, though they are inclusive of all taxes. Reservations are recommended at most restaurants.

Tourists wanting their fill of cheap eats can grab a bite at local pizzerias, food stands, cafes and bakeries rather than full meals at restaurants. You'll get a good bang for your buck by feasting on the hearty pizzas and freshly baked treats. Local restaurants serve everything from the popular reindeer meat to freshly caught seafood.

Carnivores will have a field day in Oslo owing to abundance of meat (reindeer, elk, seal and more) and fish. Those on a tight budget may have to alter their diet and exercise prudence while negotiating the menu to keep expenses reasonable. Oslo's food scene is not very vegetarian friendly. Also, drinkers will have to shell out big bucks for their daily fix. Most locals simply pick up alcohol from supermarkets to enjoy a relaxed drink at home in signature Norwegian style.

Though there are several options for eating out in Oslo, tourists mostly survive on a mix of café and picnic food. This may seem extreme though, and there are still some places where you can feast for a reasonable price. A full buffet breakfast offered at a majority of the city's hotels and hostels is a good way to fill up inexpensively. Look out for special lunch deals or combos at various places, where you can enjoy a decent meal for about NOK150.

Breakfast and Snacks

A true-blue Norwegian breakfast is an elaborate affair comprising cheese, cold meat, fish, bread, eggs and crackers, guzzled with fresh ground coffee or tea. You can enjoy a real good quality breakfast at the HI hostels and most popular city hotels that stuff you up for the entire day. Breakfast is mostly included in the room rate, like everywhere else.

Picnic basket foods such as bread, cheese, fruits and yoghurt are readily available at all supermarkets, in addition to staples (can be pricier than most European nations) for self-catering such as pasta, rice, veggies, meat and cereal. Though coffee, tea and tinned fish is reasonably priced, other tinned items can be steeply priced.

Fast food can be your best bet for a warm and bargain takeaway meal. Oslo's streets are sprinkled with hundreds of kiosks and food stalls pedaling delicious hot dogs, loaded pizza slices, chips and chicken chunks. If you are feeling a little richer than hotdogs, opt for a sandwich or smorbrod (bread crammed with heaps of garnishes, dressings and meat) as it is locally called. These can be seen seductively arranged on the windows of most Oslo bakeries or bar-cafes or what's now known as sandwich bars that have sprung up throughout the city.

You can pick up food from the local supermarkets or grocery stores and enjoy a picnic in one of the city's open parks. In summer and spring, disposable grills (engangsgrill) are sold everywhere, so you could even cook up your own meals. Though drinking alcohol is not permitted per se in public, no one minds if you are discrete, don't cause any trouble, and pick up after you.

Lunch

If you are looking for a decently priced lunch, eat during peak hours (note that the city doesn't have much of an afternoon meal culture, and a majority of the eateries do not open their shutters until late) when self-service eateries (*kafeterias*) offer daily special meal combos. This can be a fish or meat preparation with sides of mashed potato or a salad. They may throw in a drink, bread or coffee. The price ranges from NOK 150-200. These are more of a feature on the outskirts of Oslo than the main city, which is dotted with chic café-bars. You can relish a hearty meal of salads, vegetables, pasta and more at these centrally located café-bars for about NOK 160-220. Some restaurants slash their regular prices at lunch so it may be a good idea to opt for lunch over dinner if you want to experience one of the city's famous eateries. Make sure to call ahead and check if they have some special lunch discounts or you'll end up forking out big bucks.

Rice Bowl Thai Café (Sentrum), Villa Paradiso (Grunerlokka), Bagel & Juice (Slottsgate), Peppes Pizza (Sentrum), Fruhagen

(Grunerlooka), United Bakeries (Frogner), Olivia (Aker Brygge), Café Frolich (Frogner), Mogador (Toftes Gate) are some of the more affordable snack and lunch places in Oslo.

Dinner

Even though full meals can be pricey at Oslo's swanky restaurants, don't leave without feasting in an authentic local establishment for your share of succulent reindeer preparations and fresh seafood. Main courses are typically priced from NOK 200 and upwards, while starters and desserts are around NOK start from NOK 100. Sea food lovers should try monkfish and catfish. Some hotels may also offer all you can eat buffet deals from evening. A local tip is to go early and lay your hands on fresh heaps of cold cuts, pickled sea food and salads before the crowds start streaming in. There are only a handful of hot dishes such as soup, meatballs, eggs etc.

Oslo also has a huge variety of global eateries where you can tuck into delectable and fairly authentic Chinese, Japanese, Persian, Indian, Moroccan and Mediterranean treats.For a more upscale dining experience, head to Maaemo, Hos Thea, Solsiden Seafood, Fauna or Feinschmecker.

Drinks

Although alcoholic drinks are widely available in restaurants and bars, the taxes levied on them are eye popping high. The distribution of ales, wines and other spirits is stringently controlled by the state run Vinmonopolet. Visitors can enjoy drinks at cocktail bars, restaurants, open cafes and pubs. A glass of wine will generally set you back by about NOK 50. Beer (weaker beer below 4.05% ABV) is available at most Oslo shops and supermarkets. Stronger beer and spirits can be exclusively bought from the state run Vinmonopolet shops.

Vegetarian Eats

As mentioned earlier, vegetarians may not have it easy in a meat and sea-food swamped Oslo. There are a few specialist vegetarian restaurants of course, but they are more far flung and offer limited options, with some exceptions. Salads at café bars or pizzerias are your safest bet. Vegans will have it even tougher, because when Norwegians aren't sinking their teeth into the meat with gusto, they are savoring hearty cheese and yogurt creations. Take solace in the fact that unlike a lot of other European destinations, you will know what exactly you are about to eat, since English is widely spoken throughout Oslo. Self catering buffs can source their ingredients from health food stores located all over the city.

Krishna Cuisine is one of the best option for both vegetarian and vegan fans. The place is easy to miss, tucked away as it is in a tiny shopping center near Majorstua. The eatery whips up a temping array of green grub. They typically have a soup and preparation of the day. Dinner patrons can enjoy a complimentary refill if they pick the dinner of the day option. Falafel and Kabab is another good place where vegetarians can enjoy hearty falafels (fried chickpea balls) rolled into pita bread for about NOk 40.

Food Strips

St. Hanshaugen is a wonderfully buzzing foodie haunt for travelers seeking their share of tortilla chips, cinnamon buns, beetroot hummus and kinchi, topped with local experiences. This is the brick-walls, street art and organic local grub kind of place, frequented by the city's hippies.

Another emerging food district superpower is Vulkan, nestled in Oslo's uber cool Grunerlokka district (formerly an industrial hub). With amazing jaw-dropping street art and heaps of scrumptious food enticing displayed on food stalls, what's not to like about this place? Visitors can enjoy a staggering variety of food treats (basque pintxos, anyone?) from stalls peppered all over the Mathallen Hall. Anni's Polsemakeri is where the locals head to for their fill of piquant Norwegian sausages.

Accommodation

Oslo has a fairly varied selection of hotels that cater to every budget, though on an average they can be a tad too expensive than other European hotspots. That said, there are still plenty of options if you want to experience Oslo's hotels are modern, comfortable and strategically located. It houses Hotel Continental (the sole Norwegian inclusion in The Leading Hotels of the World), the heritage Grand Hotel (a prominent city landmark) and the lofty 37-storied Radisson Blue Plaza Hotel (the second tallest hotel structure in Europe). Hotel prices often include a massive buffet breakfast, which can work out to be a good deal considering the sky-high food prices.

For visitors who like to savor a more up, close and personal experience, Oslo features a nice mix of guest houses, camp sites, youth hostels, family hostels and homestays. Note that some places are open to visitors only during summer. Some year round accommodation options in Oslo include Perminalen Hotel, Anker Hostel, Bogstad Camping, Youth Hostel Haraldsheim and Oslo Hotel Central.

Prices are naturally sensitive to visitor. A double room may come to approximately NOK 1000 when it's slack, while the same may cost NOK 2000 during rush season. On an average though, NOK 1500 may cover the accommodation expenses for two in a double room throughout the year.

Oslo's increasing fame as a tourist destination has only led to a surge of travelers filling up the city's most popular accommodations, so book ahead for better choice. The city's tourist information center is the best place to head to if you haven't book ahead and need a place to stay for the night.

For a lesser anonymous option, many backpackers prefer pensions. These are tiny and more personal guesthouses, where you can hob with locals and enjoy native food treats. Rooms are typically priced at NOK 650-775 for a single and NOK 700-800 for a double. Breakfast is generally charged extra. Guesthouses and inns are other intimate accommodation options. Some of them are housed in wonderful historic premises. Amenities here are decent and comfortable, minus the luxurious trimmings. At some of the more inexpensive places, you may be required to share bathroom facilities. A few guesthouses and pensions are also equipped with shared kitchens to whip up your own meals and mingle with fellow travelers.

Hostels are the mainstay of Oslo's travel and hospitality industry. They are clean, affordable, comfortable and centrally located. Hostels can be booked online as well. On the whole, they are an excellent alternative to hotels, though you want to avoid the more institutional and lackluster school-hostels that are occupied by visitors during summer break. Prices can range from NOK 250-400/night for a single dormitory bed, which generally includes a lavish buffet breakfast at the pricier hostels.

A majority of the hostels feature a few couple and family rooms, which can cost approximately NOK 500-900/night for a double, including breakfast. Costs can be further trimmed by sharing rooms and dorms with other visitors, which may work out to an estimated NOK 70-100 per person. Renting bed-sheet and towels should set you back by another NOK 50 and 20 respectively.

Consider becoming a member of Hostelling International (HI) before booking a hostel to save on the 15% surcharge. Annual membership for HI isn't very high and you may end up saving quite a bit on your accommodation expenses. Several hostels are open only from June to August, and most are shut from 11 am to 4pm. A few also have a night curfew (11pm-midnight), though this may seem like a boon given Oslo's exorbitant carousing.

Several hostels serve warm meals post sundown for about NOK 110-140. Though they offer a decent value for money, hostel meals may vary from downright insipid to hugely appetizing. Though many hostels feature a tiny kitchen, self-caterers may have to carry their own cooking equipment. A handful of these hostels offer packed or picnic lunches for sightseers.

Oslo's tourist office can often offer you a private stay in a local's house, with kitchen facilities included at times. Prices are anywhere between NOK 350 to400/night for single and NOK 400-600/night for double. Sometimes, there's a reservation fee involved. They offer the required privacy since most these rooms are independent of the central residential structure. Some travelers prefer private residences to local hostels for better facilities and privacy. Carry a few essential utensils if you plan to cook your own meals and look for rooms with bedding if you aren't traveling with a sleeping bag.

Shopping

There's no dearth of shopping options in Oslo ranging from the pedestrian street near Karl Jones gate selling dubious goods to glamorous and high priced Aker Brygge. The chestnut tree lined Bygdoy alle is a favorite with furniture and interior design shoppers, while Bogstadveien is known for its high end merchandise (non-chain fashion stores selling chic outfits and accessories. If you are after an even more luxurious experience, head to Akersgata, which houses many exclusive and upscale shops and the plush Eger shopping centre. Steen & Strom is one of the city's earliest department stores, featuring a variety of popular clothing brands, along with a floor each dedicated to cosmetics and home décor stuff. Enjoy a cup of coffee at the store's rooftop café, offering far-reaching views of Oslo and its naturally bountiful surroundings.

Chapter 3: Bergen and Western Fjords

Encircled by the picturesque seven hills and fjords, Bergen is remarkably beguiling. The UNESCO World Heritage listed city is a captivating montage of mountains, sea and fjords. Make no mistake though, the natural elements are beautifully flanked by a bevy of chic restaurants, art galleries and a noteworthy nightlife. Straight out of fairly tale Victorian setting, Bergen features an evolving cultural life and excellent coffee and music venues, apart from a rapidly emerging food scene and an impressive art collection. Tourists can be spotted tucking into platefuls of fresh seas-food at Bergen's waterfront restaurants. Although visitors use Bergen as a base for exploring surrounding islands and the scenic western fjords, there's a lot to explore within the city. Here's all the info you need to travel in and around Bergen like a boss.

Moving Around

Bergen airport is located approximately 20 km from the south of the city in Fleshland. It is connected to the city center via the Flybussen buses that halt at Ole Pass and tourist information center, before concluding at the waterfront Radisson Blue Royal Hotel at Bryggen. The tickets are priced at NOK 100/one-way and 160/return journey. Taxi fares for the same route clocks to around NOK 350 to 400.

If you plan to use a car or motorcycle in Bergen, bear in mind that metered parking is restricted to half hour or a couple of hours throughout the city. The most popular and largest indoor parking lot is the all day long Bygarasjen, located at Bergen's bus terminal. Here you will end up forking out NOK 130 per 24 hours, whereas other places will set you back by over NOK 200.

The Vagen Harbor Ferry plies from May to August from Torget fish market to Tollbodhopen near Bergen aquarium. Use your boat ticket to get a 25% discount on the aquarium's admission fee. City buses (NOK 25 per adult) run from the center of Bergen to various destinations in and around the city. Bus no.100 plies between the central bus terminal and Bryggen.

Many tourists take the Bergen Line train journey from Oslo to Norway, which is touted to be one of Europe's most scenic rail journeys. If you want to savor the charm of Norway at a more relaxed pace, this may indeed by a soul stirring adventure. There are well-connected public transport options from Bergen station to prominent city destinations.

Attractions

Bryggen

Bergen's oldest historic quarter streams along the Vagen Harbor eastern shore in fascinating rows of wooden and stone structures. Do not miss the wooden alleys that transformed into a hotbed for local artists, with bijou shops at every corner. Soak in the atmosphere of an intimate harbor community.

Ole Bull Museum

Nestled on the pleasant Ole Bull Island, this sprawling 19th century estate was the erstwhile residence of Ole Bull (Norway's superstar violinist). Borrowing from the Moorish Granda architectural style, the structure is replete with large domes, marble columns, garden paths and lofty ceiling halls. There's a tiny in house café and grounds for leisurely walks. There's a ferry plying from Buena Quay to Ole Bull Island, operating hourly from 11am to 3pm. Skyss buses also ply infrequently from Bergin bus station to Buena.

KODE

Bergen oozes so much art that all its art museums have been bunched together into a collective KODE institution, which is one of the single largest Scandinavian art collections. A quartet of architecturally stunning and unusual structure flank the Lille Lungegard Lake, each one flaunting a unique focal point. KODE houses one of Bergen's most prestigious dining venues, Lysverket along with the charming Smakverket café. The entry ticket allows visitors access to all four structures for a couple of days, in addition to a 30% discount on the admission fare at Edvard Grieg Museum Troldhaugen.

Edvard Grieg Museum

The summer house of ace Norwegian composer Edvard Grieg, the enchanting 19th century Swiss style villa is juxtaposed between fragrant gardens and a beautiful rustic peninsula setting. Other than the house, the premises houses a contemporary exhibition center, a sprawling concert hall and one the highlights of the museum – a small lake-front Composer's Hut. There is a daily tour departing from the local tourist office from June to September at 11:30 am, which includes transport, a brief piano concert and admission fee.

Bergen Card Attractions

Like the Oslo Card, Bergen Card gives you discounted access to several tourist attractions, free travel on the Light Rail and city buses, as well as slashed prices on selected eateries and parking lots. In addition to this, you can enjoy access to several cultural events and sightseeing tours. Bergen is a mélange of museums and heritage structures, which can be conveniently enjoyed with the

Bergen Card. From taking a trip to Mt. Floyen for catching sweeping views of the city to enjoying the region's indigenous marine treasures at the Bergen aquarium to playing around with technology at the intriguing science centre, you may be able to see a lot more with a city card. Top off your day with a meal and cultural extravaganza at the one of Bergen's favorite venues.

Eating Out

Bergen features an endless supply of world class restaurants, a majority of which offer a fine selection of fresh seafood. While the more expensive tourist haunts are located in Bryggen, the marginally lower priced ones are concentrated on the back streets Bryggen, with another bunch of them nestled around Engen. Locals often eat at the affordable and informal café-bars and coffee houses, which are generously sprinkled throughout Bergen's city center.

Bergen's most iconic preparations are the fish soup and raspballer (potato dumplings served with sausages, sheep meat, butter, bacon and more). Several city cafes feature raspballer on their menus every Thursday. These are your best bet for cheap local treats. Fish balls accompanied by fish soup is also widely prevalent throughout Bergen's cafes and small eateries. Look out for treats such as pinnekjott (cured and smoked lamb meat), lutefisk (lye dried cod) and ribbe (baked ribs) near the festival season from November to January.

Budget eaters can head to Café Spesial (Christies Gate 13, which offers good food at affordable prices. Populated with the student crowd, the menu is a melange of pizzas, pastas and some middle east influenced preparations. Average price for a dish is approximately NOK 150. Hot Wok (Vestre Torggate 1) is another local crowd puller, with its reasonably priced Asian treats and filling pizzas (priced under NOK 100). Hot Wok has a reduced price lunch menu featuring house favourites in smaller portions. Ravenous late night snackers can make a beeline for the Trekroneren hot dog stand (beginning of Kong Oscars Gate), which sells incredible delicious hot dogs are humble prices. The chunky, filling rolls come in a choice of flavored sausages, which also make for a smart on the move lunch.

Naboen is one of those rare gems, where you can feast on local treats without breaking the bank. For amazingly low prices, visitors can relish large portions of Swedish meatballs (less than NOK 100) and other Scandinavian delicacies. The menu is predominantly Nordic, with some staple bar food. Naboen offers an extensive beer menu, comprising international and locally brewed items. If you are on a tight budget, sit downstairs (where the prices are lowest).

Sostrene Hagelin (Strandgaten 3 near the fish market) is a nice option for traditional sea-food takeaway. For NOK 35, you can get a bowl of sea food soup and about NOK 9 will get you a piece of scrumptious fish cake. Both locals and tourists can be spotted in droves here. Sostrene's food is known to be unfussy, healthy and top quality. Perfect for healthy eating on a budget in Bergen. Royal Gourmetburger Gin undoubtedly makes the city's best burgers.

For a more upscale dining experience, head to Lysverket, where Chef Christopher Haatuft elevates fresh seafood and seasonal vegetables into artistic creations, using a range of colors and textures. Colonialen is another 'on its way' to Michelin fine dine restaurant, whipping up Scandinavian delicacies featuring bold flavors, fresh produce and delectably unique combinations. Restaurant 1877 is charmingly housed in an erstwhile harborside building, and serves decent three or five course meals from a no-fuss list comprising cheese, dessert and fish.

Accommodation

A majority of the tips mentioned under Oslo's accommodation options also hold good for Bergen, with hotels being the most expensive options. Hostels and homestays or private house accommodations may suit more flexible and budget conscious travelers, though it all boils down to individual prices, which may vary. Bergen has a fairly good mix of hotels, which fill up pretty fast during summers and peak festival days. Some of the more well-known Bergen properties include Radisson Blue Hotel Norge (4-star), Radisson Blue Royal Hotel (4-star), Clarion Collection Hotel Havnekontoret (4-star property housed in an elegant early 20th century Neoclassical stone structure, Det Hanseatiske Hotel (4-star and the sole city hotel housed inside an original timber structure).

For hostels, your best bet is Bergen Montana Family and Youth Hostel and Bergen YMCA Hostel. The former offers decent facilities for budget travelling families. Among other facilities, it offers free Wi-Fi, a couple of well equipped kitchens and complimentary guest parking. Located bang in the heart of Bergen, YMCA Hostel features clean and comfortable rooms along with a pleasant rooftop terrace offering splendid city views.

Bergen's Beach Life

Summers in Bergen can be enjoyably spent lazing on the city's innumerable beaches. Temperatures in Bergen are comparatively warmer than other Norwegian western coastal towns. Since the outer cluster of islands protects the region from North Sea's chilly waters, the tinier bays feature more warm waters. Bergen's beaches are fresh, sultry and clean. Some of the more well-known beaches include Arboretet at Hjellestad, Kyrkjetangen and Hellenset. There are bathing houses all over Nordnessparken in Sandviken. Go hiking to Skomakerdiket, up Mount Floyen , which has a lovely fresh water beach.

Western Fjords

If there's a single image that captures the true essence of Norway's munificent natural beauty, it is the fjords. These are mammoth clefts spanning from the coast far into the sea to create a visually dazzling natural backdrop. Fjords are a combination of tranquility yet ruggedness. Tourist brochures are filled with purple prose paying homage to the beauty of the fjords, yet none of it seems overstated. They are inarguably gorgeous, especially during May, when the fjords are awash with breathtaking landscape colors. Winters too create a lovely scenic contrast of the blue-water and white snow. Thick blankets of snow envelop valleys and hills. Summers bring scores of nature enthusiasts to enjoy a variety of outdoor pursuits such as hiking and cycling.

The west coast close to Bergen is the undisputed "Gateway to the Fjords." Bergen is a great springboard for exploring the surrounding fjords. Visitors can begin at Hardangerfjord (known for its delightful fjord side hamlets) and Flamsdal valley that has the Flamsbana mountain railway going down to Aurlandsfjord. Sognefjord, decorated with picturesque villages, is Norway's longest, deepest and most fascinating fjord. Flanked by Nordfjord and Sogneford on either side is the Jostedalsbreen glacier. To Nordfjord's east is one of the country's most spectacular fjords, the rugged Geirangerfjord.

Go further north to experience the splendor of Trollstigen highway, and the towns of Andalsnes and Alesund (think attractive Art

Nouveau structures). Down South, Stavanger houses the country's most defining images – the Prekikestolen and Kjeragbolten fjords.

Top Activities For Visitors

Pulpit Rock Hike

One of the most sought after adventures in Norway's western fjord region is hiking to Pulpit rock. Towering over 600 meters, the Ryfylke attraction soars over Lysefjord.

Visitors can enjoy sweeping vistas of Lysefjod and its adjoining mountains. The hiking route is littered with lovely picnic spots and bathing areas. Note – wear a sturdy pair of walking shoes and carry walking sticks, food and winter clothes. It's a two hour hike from Preikestolgytta to Preikestolen, and the best time to enjoy it is from April to October.

The best way to reach Preikestolen during the main season is by ferry from Fiskepirterminalen in Savenger that concludes at Tau, and a bus to Prekestolen Fjellstue from where the hike commences. Another fascinating experience is viewing the fjords from a boat or car ferry from one of the several places enroute from Lysefjorden such as Stavanger, Lauvvik and more.

Visit the Folgefonna National Park

One of Norway's largest glaciers, the Folgefonna National Park is famous for its spectacular landscape comprising mountains, lakes, waterfalls and fjords. Visitors can do and see plenty of things inside the park, which makes it a significant tourist destination, though still non-intrusive and less crowded. Trails begin at Bergsto, Mosnes and Rullestad in Etne.

Take The Flobanen Funicular Railway

The Flobanen funicular ride atop Mount Floyen offers awe-inspiring Bergen views, besides featuring a kid's playground and near perfect mountain walking trails. The funicular train allows you to see the entire city of Bergen in 8 minutes flat. One of Norway's most iconic attractions, the trip commences from the city center and exits up the magnificent mountains in what could be your once-in-a-lifetime experience. The funicular drops you off at a lovely area surrounded by numerous hiking paths. Floyen also has a cafeteria, play area for children, a small souvenir shop and restaurant. The foncular operates from early morning hours until 11pm throughout the year. It is prams and wheelchair accessible. Tickets can be purchased at the Bergen Tourist Information Center.

Trolltunga

Trolltunga is a striking scenic cliff located at approximately 1100 meters above sea level, and over 700 meters over Lake Ringedalsvatnet. Hikes commence from Skjeggedal and snake through scenic mountains and lakes, covering a to and fro Trollunga distance of 23 kilometers (takes about 10-12 hours). Mid-June to mid-September is a good time to hike here, depending on when the snow starts melting. Do not attempt to hike here during winters. It can be extremely dangerous. Also, the Trolltunga hike in any season can be a challenge. Evaluate if you are fit and have dependable equipment before setting out. It isn't an easy route and no cellular phone coverage is available. Carry a map, lots of eatables and drinks, a first aid kit and a compass.

Norway's mountain weather changes rapidly, hence be sure to check the most updated weather forecast before beginning your Trolltunga expedition. Since daylight is shorter from September and nights can be extremely dark and cold, it is recommended that hikers start early in the day. Overnight hikers should carry their tents if they wish to stay atop Trolltunga. All nature based adventures are at the visitor's risk, so ensure you have everything covered before stepping here.

If you are travelling from Bergen, take the skyss bus route 930 from Bergen to Odda. From Oslo you take a train to Voss, and then bus route 990 from Voss to Odda. There is a Trolltunga shuttle service offered by most accommodation providers in Odda that drops visitors at the hike's starting point.

Day Trips From Bergen

Hellesoy in Oygarden is a beautiful island touching the North Sea on a 2-hour drive from Bergen. Visitors can enjoy hiking, fishing, extreme sports or a quiet open air cafeteria lunch here. Sea side accommodations are available for those wanting to plan overnight trips.

Voss is a lovely village located on the eastern side of Bergen, known for its action-packed adventure activities such as rafting. It hosts annual extreme sports festival known as Ekstremsportveko during summer. Voss is also superb for hiking, cycling and skiing. One of the country's most famous jazz festivals –the Vossa Jazz is hosted in March. Voss is connected to Bergen via train or the E16 route by car.

Kvamskogen is another much sought after Bergen day trip destination, especially during winters. Located about 400 to 1350 meters above sea level, it features many alpine slopes and innumerable cross country skiing opportunities. Everything from ski rental equipment to professional instructors is available at a reasonable price. There are buses plying between Kvamskogen and Bergen.

Lysoen originally belonged to legendary local musician Ole Bull. He bought it in the late 19th century and drew a plan for the home Ole himself built. Today, the island is a fantastic place for enjoying languid walks and watching the musician's remarkable house. Guided tours are conducted every hour. The island can be reached via a ferry ride from Buena quay. There is a small café and souvenir shop inside the island.

The Famous Hurtigruten Cruise

The Hurtigruten cruise is often touted to be one of the world's most scenic journeys, covering 34 ports across Norway's pristine fjord and island sprinkled coastline. The entire voyage embarking from Bergen and culminating at Kirkenes is a hop-on, hop-off affair that allows travelers to explore destinations at their own pace. The vessel takes travelers across the mystical Arctic Circle, covering an aggregate distance of around 4,000 kilometers. The vibe is flexible and informal, with visitors getting in and out of destinations to enjoy a more open itinerary.

The entire cruise takes 11 days to complete or you can just hop in and off as you wish. Many visitors prefer taking shorter trips, taking advantage of the multiple stops and daily departures along the way. These ships can also accommodate vehicles, which make them extremely convenient for people who want to combine cruise trips with visits to various destinations ashore.

One of the best parts about a journey aboard the Hurtigruten is that no two voyages on it are the same. Every ship features a distinct character that helps visitors explore a wide range of Norway's magnificent natural wonders such as fjords, waterways and picturesque ports.

While some visitors prefer taking the cruise in winter to experience the famous Northern Lights spectacle, others prefer to view Norway's scenic delights in a clearer and brighter summer landscape. The Norwegian coast's special characteristics are in their element during autumn and spring, which witnesses the most spectacular variations.

Chapter 4: The North Pole and Northern Coast

Few destinations on earth conjure up North Pole's mysterious isolation, characterized by darkness free summers and lightless summers. Though completely inaccessible a century ago, Norway's North Pole today plays host to explorers waiting to discover the natural ruggedness of ice topography at 90 degrees north latitude. Visitors can sail from Spitsbergen (the main Norwegian Svalbard archipelago island) on specially appointed boats in the mystical Arctic Basin to enjoy onboard lectures, polar bear sightings and witnessing the Arctic birds up, close and personal. Celebrations run aboard with clinking glasses of champagne when ships reach 90 degrees north to pay homage to legendary explorers who first accessed the spot. Subject to ice conditions, visitors can also enjoy walks and a dip in the Arctic waters (for the truly brave).

One of the best ways to access the Norway's northern belt is to enjoy the famous Hurtigruten cruise journey, which has been transporting enthralled passengers from Bergen to the deep echelons of the Arctic Circle. The Filigreed coastline route is replete with incandescent fjords, sky-kissing mountains, glaciers and remote villages, which can be reached only via the cruise. The streamer covers 35 ports spanning   3, 200 miles and takes 12-days for a round trip.

Svalbard

Svalbard has been the focal point for Norway's North Pole tourism. It features everything from fascinating indigenous wildlife to the arctic topography to erstwhile mining towns, which are all eerily gorgeous. Svalbard is a cluster of Norwegian islands nestled in the Arctic Ocean approximately 650 miles from the mystical North Pole. With an estimate 3000 inhabitants, it is the earth's northernmost all through the year human settlement. The focus of the economy has recently shifted from mining to scientific research and travel. Tourism has been on an upswing in the islands, owing to a thriving wildlife (polar bears are the clear crowd pullers) and unique ice adventure appeal. About two thirds of Svalbard's surface is a protected zone of innumerable nature reserves, bird sanctuaries, preserved geotopical areas and national parks. Though Svalbard has historically been engaged in whaling, mining and trapping, it has been enveloped by a sense of sustainability recently.

Most local residents occupy Longyearbyen(Capital of Svalbard Islands), the largest administrative settlement of the Svalbard islands. The community has transformed from a small village into a contemporary community that holds forth in a variety of industries and trades, with an incredibly surprising mix of cultural activities to boot. Longyearbyen's event calendar is filled with year round shows, exhibitions, festivals and live concerts.

Svalbard Weather

Though Svalbard hugs the North Pole, it is comparatively milder to other regions along the same latitude. Longyearbyen features average winter and summer temperatures of -14 degrees C in winter and 6 degrees C in summer. The lowest base temperature ever recorded in the island's history was -46.3 degrees in winter (March 1986), while the highest summer temperature was 21 degrees C. Svalbard generally features long winters with temperatures fluctuating between -20 degrees C and -35 degrees C. The region's cooling effect is amplified by the chilly winds. Summers are more fog ridden. With an annual rainfall of only about 200-350 millimeters, Svalbard is an "ice desert". Weather here witnesses rapid fluctuations, and any travel plans should be made only after checking up to date conditions.

Getting Here

Year-round daily flights operate to and fro Svalbard, with an increase in frequency during summers. Sometimes, there are several flights a day during summers. While a majority of the flights fly between Tromso and Svalbard, direct flights also operate from Oslo during peak summers. Flying duration is about 3 ½ hours from Oslo and 1.5 hours from Tromso. A well-organized shuttle service from the airport for scheduled flights takes visitors to a majority of the hotels and visitor guest houses without an additional charge.

Longyearbyen is located on the Spitsbergen Island, which is part of the Svalbard Islands archipelago, off the Norway Coast. Norwegian and Scandinavian Airlines run daily domestic flights between Oslo and Longyearbyen.

There can be several delays depending on extreme weather conditions and polar travel. Ideally, your schedule should be more flexible to accommodate these changes. Plan a more open itinerary by keeping aside a few days for polar travel delays.

The island road spans approximately 46 kilometers, though driving off-road is not permitted. Roads between community settlements are next to non-existent, with locals using mostly snowmobiles and boats during winters and summers respectively.

Boats ply regularly between the Svalbard and the mainland. Many travel companies organize safaris and trips, which generally exclude journey to and fro the Norwegian mainland. You will need other modes of transport to enter Svalbard.

Keep in mind the fact that Svalbard is not included in the Schengen zone. Hence, passports are to be carried by non-Norwegian travelers. Also, the European Health Insurance Card is invalid Svalbard. Therefore, purchasing travel insurance before making a trip here may be a good idea.

Top Svalbard Experiences

Winter season presents perfect opportunities for visitors to enjoy a range of activities including ski trips, snowmobile safaris and dog sledding. While some adrenaline rush craving passengers ascend up Svalbard's highest peaks on unforgettable ski trips, others are content with exploring the region's winter wonderland with snowmobile safaris or dog team sledding (which are generally operational from December to May). In some parts, they can be enjoyed in summers too.

Longyearbyen has a gallery featuring a nice collection of Svalbard's old maps, books, Thomas Widerberg's (photographer and music composer) slide show and an exhibition of Kare Tveter's creations. Another popular local attraction is the Longyearbyen church, which is open to visitors daily, with a Sunday service. The church sells delicious coffee and the famed Norwegian waffles on Tuesday evenings. This might be the best place to mingle with locals, and gain a better understanding of the region, and its culture.

To view the region's natural wonders, head to the Svalbard Museum. It features traces of native flora & fauna, Svalbard's hunting history and its mining legacy. Longyearbyen has a nice mix of restaurants, cafes and pubs. The highlight of your dining experiences here can be savoring a meal inside a unique trapper's cabin.

Activities and events are organized throughout the year from Longyearbyen. These include boat trips, hikes, riding, kayaking trips, skipping expeditions, snowmobile safaris, wilderness camps, barbecue nights, glacier walks, ice cave explorations, sightseeing trips, fossil hunting, weasel trips and dog sledding adventures.

Svalbard Accommodation

Longyearbyen offers a nice selection of accommodation options from cozy guesthouses to luxuriously appointed hotels. Try and book hotels a little below your stipulated budget as costs can go up due to polar travel delays. April is the peak season; hence it is advisable to book a few months prior to your trip.

The Radisson Blue Polar Hotel is a 5 star property located in the heart of Longyearbyen. It offers all amenities of a full service hotel, including wi-fi access and an in-house restaurant. The 5-star hotel is located a short walk away from most popular local restaurants, bars, sports equipment shops and souvenir stores.

Some popular Svalbard accommodation options include Svalbard Hotell, Basecamp Trapper's Hotel and Haugen Pensjonat. The Spitsbeggen Hotel along with Mary Ann's Polarigg is located about 10 minutes from the Longyearbyen's city center, while Guesthouse 102 and the Spitbergen Guesthouse is nestled around 2 kilometers in Longyear's upper valley region. Credit cards are accepted at most places through Longyearbyen and the city center has an ATM machine.

Guesthouse 102 is nestled in Nybyen in Longyear Valley's upper region. The guest house served as an erstwhile settlement for miners. Today the accommodation option is a thriving resort for worldwide visitors including explorers and scientists.

Other than this, visitors also put up in large heated tents at the tourist friendly North Pole camp. Warm air is released into the tent, while sleepers are offered everything from raised loungers to sleeping bags. Meals and drinks are prepared and served in separate pantry tents. Keep in mind that the facilities are basic, minus any luxurious trimmings.

Signature Northern Norway Experiences

Chasing the Iconic Midnight Sun

If there's anything visitors want to experience in Northern Norway other than the famed northern lights, it is the enchanting midnight sun. Norway's northern region sees around 76 midnight summer days from May to July. The number of summer nights increase as you head further north. Travelers can witness up to 24 hours of unwavering sunlight over the Arctic Circle, giving them plenty of time to explore local sights and attractions. From an adventurer traveler's perspective, Northern Norway is covers five main areas including Helgeland, Salten, Lofoten, Troms county and the North Cape.

In the Arctic Svalbard islands, the midnight summer phenomenon lasts from April to August. Travelers can enjoy everything from midnight glacier walks to head dogsled rides to experiencing up, and personal the staggeringly unusual North Pole weather.

Visitors can enjoy a variety of activities such as midnight golfing, watching the spectacular fjords in the backdrop of the tangerine midnight sun and paddling on Northern Norway's languid waters under an alluringly incandescent sunlight. Biking along the Helgeland coast, Arctic coast and Lofoten Island are other popular midnight sun pursuits.

Capturing the ethereal golden glow of the midnight sun has inspired many a photographers to set shop at the strategic view point bases all across Northern Norway. It's accentuating shades, elongated shadows and dramatic landscape offers abundant expressive photography opportunities.

Cable Car Ride at Tromso – Around 250 kilometers to Narvik's north, visitors can enjoy a cable car ride taking them 421 meters over Northway Norway's biggest city – Tromso. The rides are operational post midnight during summers in the backdrop of a sparkling sun on the Ringvassoya Island peak.

Hammerfest Viewpoint – Following the jagged path towards the old Salen cabin allows visitors to enjoy spectacular views of the Hammerfest and its adjoining islands. Catch sweeping vistas from a recently added 180 degree visitor viewing platform.

Finnmarksvidda Plateau – Finnmark is an open and large land expanse spanning 22,000 square kilometers. Here's where you get to convene with nature, while spotting native wildlife and embarking on exciting adventure treks. The region is awashed with the midnight sun.

Lofoten Islands – Lofoten is another superb base to experience Northern Norway's long and bright white nights (as the midnight sun nights are popularly referred to). It is touted to be one of nation's primary attractions, comprising jagged snow peaks and a sea washed with the mystical summer Arctic light. There are several activities that can be enjoyed here during the midnight sun days. Put up in a Rorbus (traditional fisherman's huts crafted from wood on stilts over the sea), which are rented to visitors during summers.

In Search of the Magical Northern Lights (Aurora Borealis)

If there's one thing that features prominently on the bucket list of every Norway bound traveler, it is experiencing the surreal and mystical northern lights. Drenched in natural history with a sprinkling of supernatural, the Northern lights or aurora borealis have for long been one of the world's most intriguing natural phenomenons. They are almost fairytale like in their appeal while enveloping the northern sky in hues of white, green and violet. The lights dance all across the northern sky in silhouettes of the crescent moon and sea horse.

Planet earth's greatest natural show happens when solar charged mass is released into the space due to storms. When these charged particles run into the earth's surface, they emit a strong reaction in combination with oxygen and nitrogen above the planet. This causes the dream-like aurora borealis.

Visitors can enjoy northern light spotting dogsled expeditions and snowmobile trips from Longyearbyen and other northern hotpots.

Best Places to Witness the Northern Lights

Though northern lights can also be spotted down southern Norway during increasing solar activity periods, it is best observed in the mystical Arctic Circle night sky. Most regions in Northern Norway will allow you to experience the incredible natural occurrence from October to March, though chances of viewing them are higher December onwards, when the skies are more cloudless.

Luck and cloudless skies are the two largest factors that will determine your success with spotting the aurora borealis. Tromso is known to feature quite a spectacular northern lights display. Another crucial element to be considered for witnessing the full effect of Northern Lights is to avoid artificial light in the viewing zone. Absence of man-made light ensures optimum effect of the aurora borealis in Northern Norway's night sky. The best time to view these lights is from 6pm to midnight, with the chances peaking between 10pm to 11pm.

An important consideration other than the factors mentioned above, especially for photographers, is to avoid capturing the lights in a mountain surrounded backdrop. This will prevent you from catching full, open-horizon pictures of the spectacle. Opt instead to photograph them against a vast plain (Finnamarksvidda plateau) or oceanic backdrop. A still and unfrozen (rare in North Norway) is your best bet for capturing splendid reflections.

The best places to spot them are from the jagged peaks of Lofoten Islands or over Tromso's stunning Arctic cathedral or the Northern Lights Cathedral in Alta.

Ski and Sail Svalbard Expeditions
There are many companies offering ski and sail expedition tours from Longyearbyen. Typically guests are picked up from their hotel and taken on an adventure-packed journey for a couple of days to

enjoy everything from midnight sun skiing to sailing in the Arctic's wilderness. In additional to renting out ski equipment, the tour organizers offer all onboard safety gear, an experienced local guide and shuttle from and back into your hotel. This may be your best bet for experiencing a wild, untouched snow region.

Dogsledding Adventures

Enjoy the quintessential North Pole dogsledding adventures at Bolterdalen. Encircled by mountain peaks, the dogsledding tours span Bolterndalen's riverbed, right up to the moraine hills region. Visitors can also spot reindeers here. Enjoy a cup of hot tea at the dogyard, while greeting cute sleddog pups. The activity typically lasts for 4-5 hours, with an option to self-drive a dogteam in the throes of Bolterdalens spectacular snowy wilderness.

Most tour organizers include full clothing gear, and offer basic instructions about dogsledding before embarking on the trip. While the initial trip will be undertaken with the help of an experienced guide, later trips will allow you to fasten harnesses and take the dogs to sledges on your own. One of the most memorable experiences in North Pole is going on a dogsled adventure in the backdrop of a full-moon, aurora night when the north lights are at their scintillating best in the Arctic wilderness.

Hiking in the Glacier Landscape

Start at the Lars Glacier just east of the Sarcophagus at 500 meters. Take time out to enjoy vistas above Longyearbyen and Idfjorden, before moving southward to Longyear Glacier. Witness a dramatically beautiful landscape enroute. Follow along the Longyear Glacier to reach moraine. Tour operators may offer light snacks and warm drinks on the way. Wear sturdy hiking boots and carry sufficient eatables and drinks.

Northern Norway Wildlife Spotting

Polar bears in Svalbard (around 3000) outnumber humans and can be spotted on the glaciers in Svalbard, one of the continent's most accessible North Pole patches. Go on a winter snowmobiling or skiing expedition to spot the polar bears from the boat's safety. Though these are relatively safe expeditions, there have been instances of polar bears attacking visitors. You can also spot Walruses as faraway islands of Moffen and Karl Prins Forlandet are their primary breeding grounds. They can be seen along the fjords shorelins near Longyearbyen during late spring and summers. One of the best ways to experience the region's wildlife is boat day trips near the isolated Pyramiden Russian mining zone. You can spot a nice variety of Arctic birds hovering in the region near Longyearbyen.

The elevated Arctic landscapes, dense icy wilderness and Atlantic shoreline have led to an astonishing assortment of wildlife in the North Pole region. One of Europe's most fascinating hotbed for wildlife viewing, mammals can be spotted both in their wild habitats and man-made parks such as Polar Park near Setermoen and Namsskogan Familiepark in Mosjoen's southern area.

The stunning Arctic fox is another indigenous species, which can be spotted at the Saltfjellet-Svastisen National Park, a stunning mélange of epic glaciers. They can also be seen in Borgefjell National Park in the south. In summers, they can be spotted all over the fringes of Longyearbyen's settlements.

Trondheim

Norway's former capital city, Trondheim follows closely on the heels of Oslo and Bergen as Norway's third largest city. With a pedestrian heart (think wide walking streets and plenty of open spaces) and a predominantly student population, Trondheim vibrates with life, with its mix of restaurants, cafes and museums. Boats are fervently prancing across the cityscape and seagulls can be spotted everywhere. It is busy yet surprising laidback.

The city is as known for its year round musical festivals as it for annual food festivals. Trondheim hosts music festivals in several genres including blues, rock, jazz, pop, blues and more. One of Norway's most iconic cultural and religious celebrations, the St. Olav Festival, is hosted in Trondheim.

The city streets boast of striking cycling paths that can take visitors in and around Trondheim. Take a short ride from the heart of the city to the Bymarka recreation zone, which is amazing for walking and fishing. Experience the planet's flagship bike lift in the pleasant Bakklandet town.

Another Trondheim draw is the Farmer's Market, the country's most sought after fresh produce market, where many local breweries and restaurants come together to offer a delicious local menu. With its myriad food festivals and markets, it wouldn't be an overstatement to refer to Trondheim as Norway's food capital.

Earlier known as Nidaros, the city has played a significant role in Norway's history, and houses one of the nation's most famous pilgrimage sites for around a thousand years – The Nidaros Cathedral.

Top Things To Do In Trondheim

Nidaros Domkirke

Nidaros Cathedral is the largest Scandinavian medieval structure. The west wall features a stunning mosaic of embellishments and full length statues of erstwhile kings and biblical characters. There is sublimely lit stained-glass glowing in the west end wall along with other traces of medieval architecture. The altar is above the original tomb of St Olav, the famed Viking king who reinstated the prevailing paganism with Christianity. Though visitors can enjoy leisurely strolls, guided tours are recommended. Music aficionados mustn't miss the church's splendid organ recital.

Ringve Music Museum

The musically inclined will Ringve Music Museum's pleasant appeal. Russian born Ringve was a passionate collector of usual and old musical instruments, which are today used by music students for demonstration. Visitors can browse through the old barn section with its impressive selection of global musical instruments or stroll in the peaceful and elegant 18-th century estate gardens. The best way to get here is by hopping on bus 3 or 4 and then hiking atop the hill.

Archbishop's Palace

This 12th century archbishop's home, housed adjacent to the cathedral, is one of Scandinavia's earliest secular structures. Its west wing holds the country's crown jewels. The premises also feature a museum, and a fine selection of artefacts held inside the cathedral's lower level. Enjoy the 15-minute audio visual presentation to know more about the monument's historic legacy. From June to August, visitors can enjoy amazing city views from the church towers.

Sverrsborg Trondelag Folkmuseum

Sverrsborg Trondelag Folkmuseum is one of the most fascinating local culture museums, which houses an indoor exhibition center and a collection of some the region's rarest artifacts spanning a century. There's an interesting multimedia presentation, and more than 60 period structures. Hop next door to King Sverre's castle ruins to enjoy attractive city views. Guided tours are conducted four times a day. Bus 8 from Dronningens Gate is the best way to reach here.

Hammerfest

Hammerfest's claim to fame is being the planet's northernmost town, with more than 9,000 inhabitants. None of the villages further north of Hammerfest feature a population of more than 2000 people. Other than being the northernmost town, Hammerfest is also one of the Sami culture capitals.

One of the best and cheapest ways to reach Hammerfest is From Tromso via the tiny Wideroe aircraft. There are buses plying between Hammerfest and Alta, from where visitors can take cheap flights to Oslo. Another option for scenic tour lovers is to take a catamaran from Alta, which is operational on most days. The famous Hurtigruten cruise features Hammerfest as a port of call. Hammerfest's city center is located at a 25-minute walk from the airport.

Visitors can familiarize themselves with tales of Hammerfest's destruction and post war reconstruction at the Museum of Reconstruction. The mid 20th century Church of Hammerfest is another local attraction, with its contemporary yet inviting vibe. Join the exclusive and upscale Polar Bear Club or enjoy a host of local festivals including The Arctic Open-beach Vollyball tournament or The Beer Festival (held in July). Other significant events include Music Festival (held in August) and The Blue Season Concert Festival (held in November). Another local must do is to take a ferry to Akkarfjord at Soroya Island, where visitors can enjoy adventure-packed day long or overnight hikes.

Some of the best places to put up at in Hammerfest include Thon Hotel Hammerfest, Rica Hotel Hammerfest and Hotell Skytterhuset.

Tromso

Nestled 350 kilometers above the Arctic Circle, Tromso is famous for being one of the best spots for viewing the winter Northern Lights. The small town features a surprisingly dynamic culture comprising great food, a pulsating nightlife and abundant art/history. The city houses the planet's northern most university and a fine cosmopolitan culture, earning it the moniker of "Paris of The North."

Getting In
Tromso can be conveniently accessed via plane, bus and boat. One can also reach Tromso via a memorably scenic road trip from Oslo (1700 kilometers). It may take several days, owing to Norway's unpredictable weather and tricky fjord lined roads.

Tromso is connected via domestic and international flights (about 10 daily flights) to Oslo, Svalbard, Murmansk, Arkhangelsk and Stockholm (in summers). Norwegian Airways features direct flights to London/Gatwick, which may be the most economical way to enter Tromso. Widergo operates direct flights between Bergen and Tromso. Cost conscious visitors should make the most of low summer airfares during July and August. Lots of discounted tickets can be purchased in the Northern Light period of January and February.

Though there isn't a train that goes all the way to Tromso, visitors can take buses for Tromso from the Narvik, Rovaniemi and Fauske railheads. The popular Hurtgruten ship also halts at Tromso.

Tromso has an efficient and well-connected local transport system comprising state run buses, taxi and ferry.

Aurora Watching

Tromso is often touted to be the best place in Norway for witnessing the spectacular winter Northern Lights or Aurora Borealis phenomenon. Its favorable location, backed with a host of cultural activities and entertainment options makes Tromso a tourism hot bed. The town falls in the aurora patch from around 4pm to 2 am between September to March. The best time to spot aurora borealis here is after 6, when it gets dark. December is comparatively less humid, when the chances of spotting the aurora increase dramatically. March being the driest month is probably the best time to spot the Northern Lights from Tromso. March sees abundant sunshine and lots of outdoor activities.

Local Attractions

Tromso Museum

A staggeringly large museum with several indigenous exhibits, Tromso Museum is a revelation about local Sami exhibits, Northern lights viewing equipment, Northern Norway's archeological exhibits and religious Nordic art.

Housed in an old warehouse, the Polar Museum exhibits Arctic hunting expeditions from Tromso and the Arctic region.

Visitors can enjoy half hourly cable car rides that offer panoramic city vistas from around 1382 feet above sea level. Witness Norway's famous midnight sun ride in summers and catch hauntingly beautiful images of Tromso's frosty winter landscape.

The Arctic Cathedral is one of Tomso's most photogenic buildings, with its notable stained-glass windows and fascinating mid-20th century Nordic architecture.

Visit planet earth's northernmost botanical gardens – The Arctic Alpine Botanic Garden. It has some intriguing features including a striking pond encircled by giant perennials and a section dedicated to southern hemisphere alpine plants.

Tromso Summer Activities

Packs of mountaineers are seen negotiating the Lyngen Alps and Keel range nearer to the Finnish and Swedish borders. Keep in mind that it takes careful planning, and a membership of either Troms Turlag or Den Norske Turistforeningen to go mountain climbing here. Guided glacier walks are also organized in summer.

Warm summer days sees tourists frolicking on beach Telegrafbukta, located close to Tromso Museum. Enjoy a barbeque or lazy picnic with the disposable grills available at most grocery stores in town. The more intrepid can plunge into the beach's cold waters (about 11 degrees C in summers).

Fishing is another popular Tromso summer activity. Fishing excursions by boat are the real deal, while some folks prefer shore fishing. Lay your hands on everything from coalfish to sea wolf to cod and more. Fishing trips are conducted in summers by the Tourist Information. If you'd like to be on your own, head to Hella, adjacent to the ocean at a half hour's drive from Tromso.

Hiking in and around Tromso is relatively safe and pleasant during summers. Seasoned hikers can reach Tromsdalstind starting from the central Tromso, while greenhorns can explore Floya. The mountains closest to Tromso are ideal for beginners. Troms Turlag organizes mountain refuges on the mainland at Blallkoia, North-South Trollvassbu and Skarvassbu. Non-members can put here for NOK 300/night. Visitors can make use of the wood and gag to cook meals, carry along a sleeping bag, and just leave the money there before moving.

Tromso Winter Experiences

There's more to Tromso's winter landscape than the northern lights. It's a great time for thrilling cross country trekking and skiing. The Lyngen Alps along with other Tromso mountains are the hot bed of northern Norway's winter activities including Odd piste skiing. Cetacea catamaran from the Arctic Cruises stable conducts rides from Tromso to Lyngen Alps during March and April. Visitors can also put up in huts at Lyngen.

Some of the region's most sought after trails include Snarbyeidet to Tronsdalen and Kroken. Spend the night in a DNT cabin enroute to soak up a thoroughbred cross country skiing experience. Other noteworthy trails are Raingvasoya and Kvaloya. Several ski rentals and courses are available throughout these trails.

Snowshoeing is a nice alternative for those who aren't keen on skiing. Floya, Kjolen and Rodtind can be accessed via foot or a 20-minute bus ride from central Tromso. Dog sledding and reindeer sledding can be enjoyed in Tromso, while snowmobiling activities are available in Lyngen.

Eating Out

Predictably, Tromso is a seafood lover's haven, with its variety of fresh fish and catch of the day specialties. Eating out is generally expensive like most major Norwegian cities and towns. Vegetarians and vegans will have a tough time finding a predominantly green menu in Tomso, though there are a few Oriental eateries that serve stir fry veggies, which can be the closest you can get to a whole vegetarian meal in Tromso.

If you're on a budget, avoid going to restaurants and instead grab a quick bite at local cafes. Filling café meals can cost you around NOK 100.

You can also get inexpensive food in the local town hall and university student canteens. Supermarkets offer hot food at prices lower than cafes. Feast on tacobelle (a dough with mince, cheese and tomato at one of the city's spoon bakeries or cafes). Peppes Pizza (Stortorget 2) offers a nice all you can eat lunch buffet on weekdays for NOK 100. Other budget eateries in Tromso are Grunder (Storgata 44), Yonas (Sjogata 7), Driv (Sondre3), Bla Rock (Strandgata 14-16) and Allegro (Turistvegen 19).

Some of Tromso's most popular nightclubs are Strut (Gronnegata 81), Compagniet (Sjogata 12) and Level 44 (Storgaten 44).

Local Markets

Torget Square is where visitors can fill their bags with interesting souvenirs, including Sami souvenirs and beautiful knitwear peddled by traditional Sami folks. Buy fresh turnips, strawberries and carrot from July to September. The fish port is where you can purchase shrimps and cod right off the boat. The guys here can also create handy picnics of an assortment of seafood. Just before

Christmas festivities begin, cultivators from inland valleys throng the place with native sweets.

If you are into charity and thoughtful Christmas gifting, head to Julemesse (Tromso's pre-Christmas craft fair). The area's knitting women put up their creations (tablecloth, mitten etc) for sale, and often offer the proceeds to charity.

If you are feeling more indulgent, head to Compagniet (Sjogata 12) and Emma Drommekokken (Kirkegaten 8), known for its excellent five course meals.

Day Trips From Tromso

Sommaroy is a quaint and idyllic fishing community located to the southwest of Tromso. Apart from gorgeous views of Senja and other neighboring islands, it houses pleasant beaches. Day trip buses are operational only during summer.

Go island hopping on a local ferry ride from Tromso to Belvik (50 minutes). Some of the islands you can visit include Vengsoy, Risoy, Sandoy and Vengsoy. Carry lots of food and clothes. There's no bus up to the ferry, so be prepared to arrange for your own transport.

Senja is a huge island nestled to the south of Tromso. The outer portion of the island, bearing a prominently rocky coastline, drops right into the sea for a breathtaking visual appeal. There are the charming fishing villages of Husoy, Torsken, Gryllefjord and more. In summers, ferries ply directly from Tromso to Senja. During other months, you simply drive via Finnsnes and Nordkjosbotn to access individual islands.

Made in the USA
San Bernardino, CA
29 November 2016